P9-DEZ-072

FIND YOUR STYLE

Boost Your Body Image through Fashion Confidence

SALLY McGRAW

TWENTY-FIRST CENTURY BOOKS / MINNEAPOLIS

This book is dedicated to Ellie, Addie, Olivia, Amelia, Ruby, Tillie, Evie, Astrid, Gloria, Juniper, and all of the daughters of all of my dear friends who will someday be teenagers. May you learn to love your bodies every day of your precious lives.

And to the smart, outspoken, marvelous young women who contributed their voices to this book. You are all superstars. Thank you.

Twenty-First Century Books
A division of Lerner Publishing Group, Inc.
241 First Avenue North
Minneapolis, MN 55401 USA

For reading levels and more information, look up this title at www.lernerbooks.com.

Main body text set in Bodoni Std Book 12/16.
Typeface provided by Adobe Systems.

Library of Congress Cataloging-in-Publication Data

Names: McGraw, Sally, author.
Title: Find your style : boost your body image through fashion confidence / by Sally McGraw.
Description: Minneapolis, MN : Twenty-First Century Books, a division of Lerner Publishing Group, Inc., [2017] | Audience: Age 13–18. | Audience: Grade 9 to 12. | Includes bibliographical references and index.
Identifiers: LCCN 2016009115 (print) | LCCN 2016014306 (ebook) | ISBN 9781467785693 (lb : alk. paper) | ISBN 9781512411416 (eb pdf)
Subjects: LCSH: Teenagers—Clothing. | Fashion. | Body image in adolescence.
Classification: LCC TX340 .M35 2017 (print) | LCC TX340 (ebook) | DDC 646/.3083—dc23

LC record available at http://lccn.loc.gov/2016009115

Manufactured in the United States of America
1-37921-19276-4/20/2016

CONTENTS

INTRODUCTION
CLOTHES ARE TOOLS

I used to wish I could be a brain in a jar. That's how much I hated my body.

I remember walking down the busy hallways of my high school, shuffling my beat-up Converse on the linoleum, wondering if there was a way to make my physical self disappear. I had so much going for me in the nonbody department: I got straight As, was cast in every play I auditioned for, sang in three choirs, and had a busy social life. And I was proud of my accomplishments and happy with my friendships. My insides were awesome.

But my outsides? Different story. Even though no one had ever said anything negative to me about my body, I still *heard* all sorts of negative things about it: TV commercials for weight-loss shakes; magazine ads for workout videos; and movies that showed only slim, toned female bodies. All of these things whispered to me of my inadequacies. The girls that everyone agreed were "pretty," "hot," or "beautiful" looked nothing like me. They were all tall and skinny, had flat stomachs and noticeable breasts, toned arms, and perfect skin. When I peered into the mirror, I saw a stubbornly jiggly stomach and tiny breasts, flabby arms, and gobs of acne. I looked at those beautiful girls and saw nothing of myself reflected back. I looked at them and decided that my body must be wrong. And that I should fix it.

So I dieted. For AGES. And while I was dieting, I wore nothing but loose, formless clothes that hid everything about my body. My jeans were baggy, and my shirts were stolen from the closet of my burly, 6-foot-tall (1.8-meter) dad. I picked dull colors, clunky shoes, and thick fabrics that hid my non-flat stomach and non-slender legs. I wanted to make my outside as uninteresting as possible

CLOTHES ARE TOOLS

and force people to focus on my inside. I figured hiding my body was the best way to do that.

A few years later, my girlfriend Liz mentioned that she had started wearing longer skirts to downplay her hips and something clicked inside my brain: Clothes could do something besides hide my body from view. Clothes could be tools! They could change how my body looked, even though my body was still the same inside them. As a kid, I'd worn the same things as my friends, never asking myself if I actually *liked* the clothes or felt good in them. As a teen, I'd dressed for invisibility, never trying anything that fit to my curves or drew attention. But then I saw a new, better option, and I jumped on it. It took a lot of experimenting to figure out which styles and shapes worked best for me, but eventually I found them. I started wearing flared skirts that floated over my hips, fitted tops that showed off my waist, and slim pants that balanced my proportions. My body came out of hiding.

And you know what? I felt better. I hadn't lost a pound, and I actually felt better about my body. In fact, finding clothes that worked with my body instead of against it helped me feel more connected to my physical self. My brain-in-a-jar fantasies finally vanished, and I began to see that there had never been anything wrong with my body in the first place.

Once I figured out that dressing my body well helped me feel better, I wanted to share my discovery with other women. Almost all the girls and women in my life struggled with body image, and almost all of them believed that weight change was the only way to stop that struggle. But I had found another way. It wasn't the perfect way and it certainly wasn't the only way, but it was another way besides diet shakes and weight-loss surgery. I wanted a big, open conversation about these topics. So I started a blog that focused on style as a tool for self-love and self-respect, offered judgment-free advice to all readers, and created a safe space to talk about fashion, figure flattery, and body image.

And the more I wrote and discussed and learned, the stronger my beliefs became. I know for certain that learning to dress your body in ways that feel good can increase your confidence and improve your body image. And that's what this book is all about. Seeing beauty in our bodies—right now, today, just as they are—and learning to celebrate our uniqueness by dressing our bodies with love.

Looking good and feeling good are connected. And despite what we may see and hear, there are a million different ways to look good. In fact, there are just as many ways to look good as there are girls in the world, and each of us gets to define our own unique brand of fabulous. You don't have to be tall or short or fat or skinny or pale or dark to look amazing. You just have to accept your body as it is, understand how it is shaped, find clothes that work for your specific curves and angles, and wear them with pride.

So let's get started.

CHAPTER 1
MEDIA MESSAGES

Let's start with the basics. You've had your body since birth, even though it has grown and changed since your diaper-wearing days. And although you may not have done it on purpose, you've developed a set of thoughts and feelings about your body as you've grown. Some of these thoughts and feelings are based on things such as your hair color and texture, your skin tone, your shoe size, your height, and your anatomy. And some of them are based on your own ideas and opinions or ideas and opinions you've heard others express. You've taken all of this information and created a body image for yourself: a picture in your mind of how your body looks that's related to but sometimes not the same as how your body looks to other people.

The next assumption: You watch a little TV, listen to music, and watch the occasional movie. You might also post photos to Instagram or page through a magazine once in a while. And this means you are exposed to the media—a group of industries that creates and distributes information and entertainment.

What do the girls and women you see in the media look like? Do the women you see on TV look like you? Do the women you see in magazines look like your friends or neighbors? Do the women who star in your favorite movies look like your teachers or parents? In some cases, yes. But most of us know only a couple of girls who look like Hollywood starlets. Even though women come in a mind-blowing variety of shapes and sizes, the women we see in the media tend to look remarkably similar to one another. Most of them are slender and muscular, they have long hair and perfect skin, and the vast majority of them are white European Americans. Just a few years ago, even fewer women of color, plus-size women, older women, and

Actress-model Dakota Fanning poses for a fashion shoot in the south of France. Fanning's looks are representative of the values of mainstream American fashion and style: pale, slender, European American, and blond.

MEDIA MESSAGES

gender-fluid individuals were represented in mainstream media. Seeing diversity become more of a priority for casting directors and modeling agencies is encouraging. But we've still got a long way to go, and usually the women we see in the media don't accurately reflect the women we see in our lives. And depending on how we're wired, that can have a strong impact on how we feel about beauty and bodies and self-worth. As eighteen-year-old Olivia in Georgia says, "I don't think I've ever been the girl to want to look like a specific female celebrity, but I do feel that many celebrities present unrealistic expectations of what someone should look like."

STARS OF THE SILVER SCREEN

Plenty of actresses are short or fat or old, and you'll see them on TV and in the movies. But usually you won't see them in leading lady roles. They'll be in the background, playing best friends or quirky neighbors instead of main characters. Those lead roles consistently go to white European American women who are slender and muscular, have long hair and perfect skin, and are conventionally feminine. And since most of us would rather be the hero than the sidekick, we focus on the women in those lead roles. Many of us agree that they are beautiful, and since they all tend to look the same, we start to believe that there is only one way to be beautiful.

WHY DOES THIS HAPPEN?

If you watch a classic Hollywood movie such as *The Seven Year Itch* (1955) or *Tales of Manhattan* (1942), you'll see that the lead actresses are shaped differently from the stars of the twenty-first century. Back then, they were much curvier, with bigger busts and less muscle definition. If you YouTube an episode or two of *Charlie's Angels*, a popular TV show from the 1970s, you'll see that those lead actresses also look quite different. They have fewer defined curves with an emphasis on being tall, slim, and small busted.

The American ideal of beauty and what a beautiful woman should look like have changed over the years, and it will continue to change. Social media is pushing back hard on many fronts against the idea of a single type of beauty. Plus-size model Tess Holliday's Instagram campaign @EffYourBeautyStandards encourages posters to celebrate beauty in all sizes and forms. Fashion blogs such as *Haute Hijab, The Muslim Girl, Pretty Cripple,* and *Manufactured1987* showcase women of diverse faiths, abilities, and skin colors strutting their stylish stuff. Blogs including *Black Girls Killing It, dapperQ,* and *Genderfork* along with YouTube channels such as Gigi Gorgeous create havens for people of color and gender-fluid and transgender individuals to swap shopping tips and show off amazing outfits. Stepping up to challenge norms are petite and tall women; older women; women who love cosplay or goth; and women with more tastes, body types, cultural backgrounds, and gender identities than you could imagine. If you want to see the definition of beauty exploded, look online.

Marilyn Monroe starred in a popular 1955 film comedy called *The Seven Year Itch.* Monroe is one of the most famous American female sex symbols of all time. In the 1950s, a full, curvaceous figure such as hers was viewed as desirable and sexy, not as overweight or too curvy as it might be in the twenty-first century.

MEDIA MESSAGES

But when it comes to mainstream, big-budget media, we still see a very narrow definition of beauty. And it's hard to say if movies and television are creating that definition or just reacting to it. Is Hollywood showing us thin, muscular women to shape our ideas about beauty, or are those women cast because so many people already agree that they're beautiful?

"Actresses have definitely gotten thinner over the course of my lifetime. . . . For young girls, what does that say? You need to look this way to be successful? That's not true."

—Zooey Deschanel, actress and model

Either way, women in TV and film are expected to be thin and toned even if the male actors they're working with aren't. And as time has gone on and our ideas about beauty have changed, actresses have gotten thinner and thinner. Even though superthin women don't accurately reflect what most real women look like, we admire them and want to be more like them. They're thin, so we want to be thin too. Seventeen-year-old Jenna in Minnesota comments,

If I'm watching a film and there's a scene where the girl is taking off her shirt or something, and you're like whoa, my body doesn't look like that. So you're kind of thinking while you're sitting there watching TV eating chips like oh man, what am I doing? You're just looking at this girl who's super attractive, and if you go look in the mirror it kinda brings you down. People might say, "Oh, I'm not trying to look like that, I'm just trying to be healthy." But subconsciously? You're trying to get to that image. At least that's what I think I'm doing to myself.

TURN IT UP

Women musicians may strive to look as thin and beautiful as their actress counterparts, but many of them also feel pressured to dress and act sexy. In music videos, on the red carpet, and in magazine photos, you are likely to see popular women singers wearing clothes that show a lot of skin or striking poses that make viewers think about sexual acts.

Singers and musicians often seem more like regular people than actresses. We hear their music every day, see their faces everywhere, and they begin to feel like friends. Singers and musicians are also undeniably cool and visibly powerful. So we feel connected to them and want to be more like them. Since they dress sexy, should we? Does dressing sexy help women become successful, powerful rock stars? It can definitely feel that way.

WHY DOES THIS HAPPEN?

Research has shown that songs about sex sell well, and women musicians are encouraged to write those songs and dress in sexy, revealing clothing that reflects the lyrics they're singing. Some musicians enjoy the power and sense of freedom that dressing sexy can bring, but others feel pressured to show their bodies. Since musicians need to sell songs and concert tickets to make a living, and since they are told by their managers

Kelly Clarkson is a fabulously successful singer, songwriter, and actress, who got her start in 2002 when she won the first season of *American Idol*. Since then she has earned three Grammy Awards, three MTV Video Music Awards, twelve Billboard Music Awards, four American Music Awards, and two Academy of Country Music Awards. Yet she is still subject to stinging criticism about her weight. She counters, "It's like, you're just who you are. We are who we are. Whatever size."

and record labels that showing skin will help make those sales, many women musicians end up baring more than they'd like to. And just as we may want to be as thin as the actresses we admire, we may also want to be as sexy as the singers we admire.

COVER GIRLS

Pick up any teen fashion or women's magazine and look at the cover. There's a better-than-average chance that one of the headlines will have to do with weight loss, working out, dieting, or dressing to look slimmer. According to these publications, being thin and toned is very important.

Then open the magazine. You probably know that nearly all photographs that show up in magazines—including both the advertisements and the images created for stories—have been Photoshopped to get rid of bulges or wrinkles or to reshape body parts so they are either smaller (hips) or bigger (breasts). But this awareness

Logos featuring female characters have become thinner over time. For example, Miss Columbia (also known as Lady Columbia) of Columbia Pictures had a curvaceous figure in the film studio's 1940 logo *(left)*. By the twenty-first century, she had lost her curves in favor of a slimmer, boyish figure *(right)*.

can be challenged as you're flipping through the latest issue of *Glamour*. Seeing girl after girl with long, thin legs and toned abs and perfectly round breasts can be kind of hypnotic. And it can also make you feel an emotional tug, like maybe your body would be better with longer legs and tighter abs and bigger breasts. Fourteen-year-old Grace in Chicago says, "I understand that many of the women in the photos have been Photoshopped, but it sometimes gets in my head and makes me think that I would be better looking if I lost weight, or if I spent more time worrying about what I wear."

Most magazines for teen girls and women talk about trends, shopping, figure flattery, and other fashion-related topics. So you're bound to see some ads for jeans and articles about the "must-have" items of the season as you page through. Although none of these articles says it directly, they imply that the reason you must go out and buy this handbag or that pair of boots is to fit in. Magazines publish lists of fashion items that are "in" and "out," encouraging us to ditch certain clothes and replace them with others. Many of us fear being an outcast, and few of us want to be seen wearing something that's out of style. So, in an effort to blend in and belong, we may try to buy and wear what we think everyone else is wearing.

> "I'm insecure because I have to think about what I look like every day. And if you ever are wondering, 'If I have thinner thighs and shinier hair, will I be happier?' You just need to meet a group of models, because they have the thinnest thighs and the shiniest hair and the coolest clothes, and they're the most physically insecure women probably on the planet."
>
> —Cameron Russell, Victoria's Secret model

Eighteen-year-old Sontra in Minnesota sums it up: "The magazines tell you to value looking beautiful, being fit, and being stylish."

Some of the articles and gobs of the ads will tell you all about your "flaws" and "imperfections," aspects of your body or skin or appearance that need to be changed and improved upon, according to the magazine. You may see an article that talks about a style of skirt that will make you look 10 pounds (4.5 kilograms) lighter or an ad for makeup that will make your skin's pores invisible. Some of these ads and articles will bring up things that you didn't even know were "wrong" with your body. And then they will tell you all about the product you can buy to fix your body's errors.

WHY DOES THIS HAPPEN?

Magazines and advertisers hire thin models because being thin is a big part of being beautiful, according to the fashion industry. Magazines also aim to be aspirational: they create a fantasy world by showing you images of people you wish you looked like wearing things you wish you could afford. And the magazine executives hope you'll make that fantasy a reality one day because of one thing: money.

You might think that magazines make money by selling subscriptions and single copies at newsstands, and they do. But more than half of the money magazines earn comes from the ads they sell. Advertisers want to sell their products—makeup, clothing, and shoes— and are more likely to place ads in magazines that encourage their readers to buy new, trendy, fashionable stuff. The magazine editors and salespeople know this, and they do their best to write stories and create photos that will lure advertisers and tempt readers to buy their products. The editors and staff writers may do so by presenting visually gorgeous photos or by writing positive reviews of clothes or makeup. But they may also do so by convincing you that there's something imperfect or wrong with your body and by suggesting that buying specific clothes or cosmetics will help you look and feel better.

The magazines want you to buy so they can continue to sell ads, and the advertisers want you to buy so they can continue to sell products. So why do magazines show us thin women wearing designer clothes? Because the image of the thin model makes us question our own beauty and yearn to look more like the figure we see on the page. And when we feel bad about ourselves, we just might go out and buy some stuff to make us feel better—and look more like the model.

ONLINE LIFE

Even if you don't read magazines, you're likely to see hundreds of photos every day on Instagram, Facebook, Snapchat, and other social media. These sites share photos of celebrities and real people. On social media, you are more likely to see images of more varied and diverse people than you will on TV or in print, especially if you do a little hunting for sites and accounts that focus on fashion for people who look like you, are the same size as you, or have other identity overlaps with you. But the images can still mess with your head. How others react—or don't react—to the selfies you post can have a huge impact on your feelings too.

If you post a photo of yourself and no one clicks Like or comments, that can sting. But if you post a photo of yourself and

Leomie Anderson, a famous young British model, founded a fashion blog called *Cracked China Cup* where she discusses style, fitness, and her life as a model. In the summer of 2016, she wrote an open letter on her blog to her young female fans around the world about the issues of sexual pressure, consent, and the right to say no.

Posting selfies can be a great way to share fashion tips and to see other girls that share your interests—and body type. Use social media as a way to boost your sense of style and self-confidence. Talk to a trusted friend or adult if that's not your experience. Work together to find all the awesome places girls like you hang out online!

get negative comments, that can feel like a punch in the stomach. This can feel so much more real than anything about movie stars or fashion models. This is your life, your school, and your friends. And even though getting caught in the cycle of posting selfies, waiting for comments, and then feeling anxious or bad about them is definitely damaging, it can be hard to resist. Sixteen-year-old Alisha in Pennsylvania says,

> I would purposely post really, really ugly selfies because in a way it made me feel good about myself. But soon I started just to post beautiful ones and left the ugly ones only for my best friend. I didn't really notice until my friend said I look like a model in every single photo. After that I started to ask myself, "Am I really THAT girl?! I became that girl that I desperately didn't want to become!" So I posted an ugly photo. Then I

deleted the photo because I was scared of what others thought of me. I was ashamed of myself and I was mad at myself just because of some stupid photo I deleted.

Looking at photos that others have posted can stir up negative feelings too. When you see girls who look different from you getting positive comments about how hot they look, it can make you question your own beauty and test your self-confidence. When you see girls who look similar to you getting negative comments about their looks, you may transfer that negativity onto yourself.

WHY DOES THIS HAPPEN?

Your phone goes with you everywhere, right? You can leave magazines at home and you probably don't watch movies every night, but social media is with you wherever you go. And that you get instant feedback from people in your life whose opinions matter makes your social media interactions extra powerful. Looking at your friends' photos and reading the comments may make you feel that if you don't look a certain way, you'll face ugly consequences: anything from bullying to being unpopular to never finding someone cute to date. And when you're constantly worrying about those things, it can be hard to feel good about yourself.

WHAT CAN YOU DO?

Experts point to one simple thing you can do to combat the negative effects the media may have on your self-image. Be aware.

Some publications and websites do a fantastic job of showing and celebrating diverse women. *Bust* and *Bitch* are two great magazines that have always highlighted women of size and women of color. *Bustle* is an online magazine that covers transgender fashion and identity as well as runs stories on plus-size women and women of color. The *Mary Sue* site focuses on geek culture and talks about how women are represented in TV, movies, comic books, and other media. Many other social media sites are well worth exploring, especially if you feel excluded from mainstream media.

But if you do find yourself paging through a magazine or watching a television show that has absolutely no one that looks like you, be aware of what's happening and why. When you compare yourself to actors and start to feel bad, be aware that those people have large staffs whose only jobs are to make the actors look amazing. They have chefs, personal trainers, stylists, tailors, and more. Actors are professionally pretty or good looking. Remember that before you start to tear yourself down.

Mainstream fashion media is slowly widening the lens to more routinely include women of all shapes, sizes, origins, and gender identity. This young woman uses jewelry, lacy cuffs, and an elegant braided hairstyle to add flair to her comfortable, casual outfit.

When you see your favorite musicians dressing sexy, be aware that they are under tremendous pressure to do so. They are constantly in the public eye, and how they look can have a huge impact on how popular their music becomes. Remember that you can be inspired by them but that you don't need to imitate them.

Be aware that the ads and images of thin, toned men and women in magazines have been created to make you feel bad about yourself so you'll spend money to "fix" yourself. And also that almost all of those photos have been changed and digitally manipulated to create a certain type of "perfect" body. Remember that you don't need to be fixed for any reason.

When you receive or see nasty comments online, be aware that it's easy and cowardly to hide behind a computer to tear down your friends and peers. Remember that people who are doing that probably feel pretty bad about themselves and are taking it out on you. And always know that you can and should report abusive or threatening posts of any kind to your principal, school counselor, a parent, or any other trusted adult.

Keeping these things in mind is part of practicing media literacy. It helps you build the knowledge and strength to resist the confining, shaming messages you hear and focus on your own uniqueness and beauty.

CHAPTER 2
STYLE AND BODY IMAGE IN REAL LIFE

Head over to your closet, and throw open the door. When you peer inside at your clothes and shoes, your first thoughts probably aren't about fashion models and movie star bodies. But they might be about the comments you'll get if you wear that red sweater *again* this week. How the people around you dress, look, talk about style, and talk about bodies may influence your thoughts and feelings even more than what you see in the media. You may do it alone, but getting dressed is definitely a social activity.

FITTING IN VS. STANDING OUT

When you shop and dress, your decisions will probably focus on one of two goals: blending in with your friends or standing out from the crowd. Neither of these goals is better or worse than the other. Dressing in unusual, original outfits can be a fun way to express yourself. Dressing similarly to your friends can help you feel connected and accepted. There's room in the world for people who do both. Fifteen-year-old Wrenna in Oregon says:

When you get dressed in the morning, you may be thinking about what other kids in your class are going to be wearing. Or you may be thinking about the activities you have planned for the day. Sometimes clothing choices are practical, while other times they are about making a statement or fitting in. Think about what makes sense for your day as you choose your outfit.

I used to dress to fit in at my previous school, but not at my current one because the reason I came to my current one is to get away from all the bullying and stuff. I feel like I can be myself without wanting to get attention.

YOUR STYLE PERSONALITY

If you prefer to dress like your friends, are confined to a dress code, or just aren't sure if you want to fit in or stand out, these are some simple, subtle ways you can express yourself through style:

Jewelry. Wear a necklace you made over the summer, a bracelet your big sister gave you when she left for college, or earrings you bought on vacation. Wearing pieces that represent people, events, or things that are significant to you lets a little bit of your personality peek through.

Hairstyles and accessories. Your hair is completely unique, and how it's styled subtly impacts your overall look. Pick a cut that makes you feel confident and grounded or bold and different. (Remember: Hair grows back.) Learn to do fishtail and French braids, play with flat irons and curlers, experiment with relaxers or let your hair go natural, add headbands and barrettes, or try extenders or box braids.

Makeup. Unless your school, faith, culture, or family has rules about wearing makeup, you can have loads of fun experimenting with different applications and styles. Lip color is often the easiest, and you can try everything from pinks and reds to bolder oranges, edgy burgundies and blacks, or funky brights such as blue or purple. Eye makeup can also be colorful or even sculptural if you learn how to use eyeliner to draw elegant shapes on or around your lids. And don't forget nails! Look online for hundreds of tutorials for nail art and creative manicures.

Shoes. A study conducted in 2012 concluded that you can accurately guess most people's personality traits just by looking at their shoes.

Small touches can add flair and personality to a simple or super-casual outfit. For example, try red—or any other emo color—for your bangs to add splash to your look.

Red lipstick is an easy way to carry through the bright, eye-catching look of this outfit.

Towering heels and giant wedges might be right for some people, but plenty of other shoe styles can help you express yourself. Think about studded Chuck Taylors, broken-in combat boots, bright pumps or tennis shoes, embellished ballet flats, sleek riding boots, or pared-down sandals. Let your feet do the talking.

Color choices. If your friends wear a specific style of sweater or head scarf, you can fit in by choosing the same style but still carve out some individuality by choosing your favorite color. If you want people to know that you're more about journaling in graveyards than cheering at pep rallies, stick to a dark, neutral palette of colors. If your culture embraces bold shades and mixed prints, incorporate those into your daily outfits. If you're a romantic at heart, try dusty pastels.

A pair of red sneakers can make an entire outfit. The sailor-striped top adds a breezy, fun feel.

How do all of these responses relate? They aren't defensive or aggressive. Instead, they focus on your individual power and decisiveness. They are playful and fun while also confident and honest. And they are all phrases that will likely put a stop to a teasing line of questioning.

AGE-APPROPRIATENESS AND SOCIAL DRESSING

You may have noticed that fashion is full of rules. Tall girls shouldn't wear heels. Fat girls shouldn't wear horizontal stripes. Short girls shouldn't wear maxi skirts. Blah-blah-blah. It's helpful to know how your dressing choices affect your silhouette, and that can mean rethinking these rules. But you will not be given detention, sent to jail, or burst into flames if you break them. Fashion rules are really just guidelines. Learn them, understand them, and then decide if you want to follow or break them.

Most fashion rules have to do with figure flattery. Some have to do with age. For example, some people believe that older women should never wear graphic tees and that younger women should never wear low-cut dresses. In reality, each individual woman gets to decide what feels good to wear at any age.

However, your dressing choices do contribute to your identity, and as a young woman, you are in the process of understanding and shaping that identity. So it can be important and valuable to understand why you want to make specific dressing choices, especially choices that other people may view as inappropriate for your age.

The main thing that riles people is when teens dress in sexy or revealing clothes. Cleavage-baring necklines, tight dresses or pants or tops, visible lingerie, short skirts, and other revealing clothing when worn by teen girls make many adults cringe. An estimated 58 percent of public schools and 71 percent of private schools enforce strict dress codes, and twenty-two states have laws governing student clothing choices. So these cringing adults aren't just blowing hot air. They feel so uncomfortable when they see teen girls in sexy attire that they have built rules around which clothes are acceptable and which ones aren't. Since these rules and dress codes often talk about girls in sexy clothes as a distraction to other students, many of them focus almost exclusively on what girls can and can't wear.

Boys have to pay attention to what they wear too, depending on where they are going. And if they choose to wear clothes—such as skirts or dresses—that are traditionally associated with girls, they may get teased or bullied. Gender-neutral and gender-flexible styles are gaining acceptance, but people who wear them often deal with fear and discomfort from the people around them. To some extent, everyone will deal with social challenges when dressing because what we wear is the first thing about ourselves we show to others.

But generally, boys aren't scrutinized and policed as closely for what they wear as girls are.

Gender-flexible clothing is becoming more popular in the United States and elsewhere. Fashion designers are showing dresses and skirts for men on the runway, and guys are wearing them for everyday wear too.

Boys have fewer clothing choices overall, and most of the garments they're offered aren't designed to be purposely revealing or tight. Girls are judged more harshly and generally have to be more careful in making choices about what they wear. Schools and workplaces and social gatherings have expectations for what is appropriate to wear and what is not, and many of them apply to both boys and girls. But girls' choices are more likely to get people—especially adults—worked up.

Fifteen-year-old Adah in Minneapolis shared this observation about her school's dress code:

> Last year we had a principal who tried to outlaw yoga pants and short shorts, things that are typically female clothing. So the football team wore short shorts and yoga pants one day. I saw more than I would have liked to!

Many people feel this double standard is wildly unfair—and sexist. For so many reasons. Some girls with big busts are likely to naturally show cleavage in anything lower cut than a turtleneck. Some girls whose skirts fit within school guidelines still get sent home for dress code violations. Part of the reason this happens goes back to the media. After seeing female-shaped bodies shown in sexy clothes and suggestive positions so frequently, many people automatically believe that female bodies are sexy and suggestive no matter what. So even when girls are technically following dress codes, if their natural body shape makes an adult uncomfortable, that adult may ignore the rules and punish the girl. And perhaps most important, these girl-only rules shift the shame. Blaming girls for being sexually distracting puts all the responsibility on girls and none on the people looking at and interacting with them. So, if some people act inappropriately toward girls wearing short skirts, it's perceived to be the girls' fault for wearing short skirts, not the fault of the people who did not control their actions or reactions.

HOWEVER. Although dressing sexy isn't fundamentally bad—no matter what dress codes may imply—it's worth examining the motivations for dressing this way. If you're someone who enjoys wearing sexy outfits, ask yourself why. Is it because it feels good to do something that gets a rise out of parents and teachers? Is it because you want to show people that you're proud of your figure? Is it because you get lots of attention when you dress sexy? Why is it important to you?

If you love the look of a short skirt, remember that any figure can rock this style. Tighter versions may feel more revealing, but an A-line skirt (slim at the waist and flaring slightly from there) flatters almost any figure, even when it's quite short.

You can use fun color combinations to draw attention away from the length of the skirt. Or think about pairing your short skirt with leggings or patterned tights. And don't forget to consider what's appropriate. If you're going to a job interview, a short skirt may not be the best choice.

Sexuality is natural. It is not shameful or dirty or bad. But it doesn't have to be something that you share with everyone or something that you show off on a daily basis. Sexuality can be private, and sexy dressing can be something you reserve for specific people and situations. It doesn't make you any less cool or powerful to save it for some places and not for others. In fact, you may find that dressing sexy feels even better when it's for a special occasion instead of every day. Alisha wisely says, "Being sexy and dressing sexy I feel are two different things. Even though you don't dress in short skirts and all that doesn't mean you can't be sexy."

You can control what to show and what to keep private, what to share and what to hide, and which parts of your personality you will express through style and appearance. What you can't control is how others react to what they see. When you dress sexy, some won't care or notice, some may be upset or unnerved or disapproving, some might think it's awesome, and some might decide that your outfit means you're looking for someone to make out with. Some dressing choices prompt unexpected reactions and behaviors, and dressing sexy can occasionally create unsafe or unwanted interactions. That's wildly unfair. You shouldn't have to be responsible for how other people interpret your looks. Yet often safety trumps fairness.

When making decisions about what to wear, consider the company, location, culture, situation, and motivation. If you know it will be safe to dress sexy, go for it. But if you risk unwanted sexual advances or if it's just plain inappropriate or insensitive or even against the rules, choose a different type of outfit. As fourteen-year-old Mollie in Brooklyn says, "I try to wear stuff that I'm comfortable in and that fits my body. I don't dress 'sexy' for parties and the like because I don't think I'd be comfortable putting myself out there like that."

IT'S ALL ABOUT YOU

Your friends' opinions and your school's dress code and the social expectations in your hometown will influence your dressing choices. You may have different abilities that make certain styles tough to wear, your size and shape may direct your choices, or your faith or culture may impact the pieces you can add to your wardrobe. You may want to wear clothes designed for a gender different from the one you were assigned at birth, or you may want to wear clothes that are bolder, funkier, or darker and edgier than the ones your classmates wear. But you make the key choices that shape your own style. Even with parameters, or limitations, you pick the clothes that hang in your closet, you create outfits from them, and you wear them. Think about how much power that gives you. And remember that people may get dressed to keep warm and avoid getting arrested for indecent exposure, but we also do it to express who we are. Olivia says, "I do keep up with trends, but if I don't like one, then I won't wear it. Style is a way for me to express myself, so I want my outfits to always represent who I am."

So what is your outfit going to say about you today?

Comfort and ease of movement are part of this woman's fashion statement. She also adds a fun splash of color through her hair accessory.

CHAPTER 3
FIGURING OUT YOUR FIGURE

Has anyone ever told you that you're a pear? An apple? A string bean? Long ago, some food-obsessed style expert created a system for classifying female bodies, and it has stuck around for ages. Once you figure out which fruit or vegetable your body most closely resembles, you're supposed to use that information to decide which clothes will flatter it. Or that's the idea.

But in real life, most of us don't fit neatly into just one of these categories. We might be mostly pear-shaped but a little bit string bean. Or we might have an hourglass shape that also has some apple-like tendencies. Adah says, "The ads really get me with 'if you have this shaped body, wear this stuff' because anyone should be able to wear anything."

So let's talk about understanding your figure without comparing it to anything or anyone.

THEORY OF RELATIVITY

To understand your figure, look at it—for more than ten seconds—in a full-length mirror, and while wearing something formfitting or possibly just your underwear. Peering into your closet

Wearing clothes that feel good, fit well, and look good—and that match your personality—are what style is all about. This young woman matches her nail color to her tattoo, both of which contrast nicely with the cool colors of her dress.

might not summon images of celebs in bikinis, but this little exercise might. So, when you do this, remember your body is unique and you can work with it in many different ways and in any way that makes you feel confident and good about yourself. You can understand your body shape without comparing it to anyone else's.

Take a long, hard look at yourself. Be as scientific and nonjudgmental as possible as you note your features. What would

FIGURING OUT YOUR FIGURE

you say defines your figure? What's biggest? What's smallest? What's distinctive or unusual? Pay special attention to how your features relate to one another. For instance, you may not think of your waist as being small on its own, but is it small compared to your hips? Are your legs long compared to your torso? Is your bust small in relation to your overall height? Comparing your body to someone else's body doesn't actually teach you anything. When you're in the fitting room trying on jeans, it doesn't matter if your thighs are bigger or smaller than Taylor Swift's. It only matters how they fit into the overall puzzle of your unique figure. So compare your body to itself and jot down what you see.

EASY AS ONE, TWO, THREE

Figuring out which clothing styles will work for your body will take some time and experimentation, but the essentials of figure flattery are actually quite simple.

1. **Wear clothes that fit you.** Avoid overly baggy, long, or oversized clothing. If clothing sags, bags, bunches, or poofs out, it's too big. Also avoid anything that's too tight. If your clothing pulls, pinches, or digs into your body, it's too tight. So is anything that shows the contours of individual muscles or the outlines of your undies.

Why is this important? Clothing that fits your body is a visual illustration of your self-awareness and self-acceptance. Seeing people who have actively chosen to wear clothing that are too loose or too tight makes us think that they aren't aware of the shape and size of their bodies. Or when we see people wearing clothing that are clearly much too large and loose, we may reason that they are ashamed of their bodies and want to hide them inside voluminous clothes. Even if these decisions are intentional, they often read as, "I don't understand my body, or I hate my body, so I wore this."

If your culture or faith requires specific garments that have more volume by nature, this may not seem to apply. But you can still make sure your clothes complement your figure. If you can use a belt to show your waistline or are able to show your wrists, both can give a visual sense of your shape and proportions. If covering your bottom half with loosely fitting garments is the priority, think about a slightly snugger top. And if you're able to layer, putting a long-sleeved but structured jacket or blazer or sweater on top will define your figure to the observing eye.

2. **Wear clothes that feel good.** Uncomfortable clothes and shoes can be distracting to the wearer. Dealing with a super-itchy sweater or a tight waistband that digs into your midsection will just make you miserable. You don't need to wear sweatpants and leggings and baggy sweaters nonstop, but you also don't need to wear anything that causes you pain or physical irritation.

Bear in mind too that there can be a difference between "clothes that feel good" and "comfortable clothes." Clothes that feel good may do so because they feature gorgeous colors or prints. You might enjoy the texture of the fabric against your skin. Wearing certain items may remind you of favorite people or places. Clothing can feel good to wear for many reasons.

Why is this important? There's a definite connection between looking good and feeling good, but it goes both ways. If you feel good in what you're wearing, you'll be more likely to hold your head up, you'll exude serenity, and you'll walk taller and smile more. Confidence is one of the best beautifiers, and feeling good in your clothes gives your confidence an instant boost.

3. **Wear clothes that flatter your body.** Clothes that flatter your body help you highlight what you love about yourself. That can mean showing off your legs in skinny jeans or your waist in belted dresses, framing your gorgeous face with a colorful hijab, or picking clothes to create proportions that please you. They also help you look good and feel confident. And to create a personal style that really works, you need to understand how your body interacts with clothing.

WHAT ARE FIGURE-FLATTERY PRIORITIES?

When you dress, you make decisions about how you're presenting your body. You may want to highlight some aspects of your body and downplay others. Those are your figure-flattery priorities.

If you crack open a magazine or go online, you'll get the impression that all women should have the same figure-flattery priorities: make your waist look smaller, your legs look longer, and your breasts look bigger, and do everything in your power to look thin. Some of those priorities may resonate with you, and that's fine. But what those magazines aren't saying is that each woman gets to pick her own figure-flattery priorities, and they may be quite different from the standard set.

Say you've got broad shoulders. Fashion magazines and websites will tell you to wear outfits that balance your figure. But if you love your broad shoulders, you may want to wear clothes such as boatneck tops, structured jackets, and big scarves that highlight or even exaggerate them. And if you want to do that, you absolutely can. YOU get to pick what you love about your body. YOU get to decide what to highlight. YOU are in charge of your figure-flattery priorities. Alisha tells us, "I have really big hips because I'm Italian, and I have a little bit of a stomach. So essentially I'm bottom heavy. But don't get me wrong. I love my body the way it is. I feel that at this point I'm not super skinny, and I'm not super big. I feel that I'm just right."

Wearing bright colors is one way to flatter your features and to draw attention to the parts of your overall look that you want to highlight. This bright head scarf, for example, draws the eye immediately to the face.

WHAT DO YOU LOVE ABOUT YOUR BODY?

How do you pick your priorities? Start by asking yourself, "What do I love about my body and want to show off?"

FIGURING OUT YOUR FIGURE

You can start with broad strokes. Do you love your height? Your strong arms? Your curvy hips? Your legs? The shape of your collarbone? The way your shoulders slope?

Don't limit yourself to the big, obvious body parts. Explode the definition of what can be included. Do you love your hair color or texture? Your ankles? Your skin tone? Your eye color? Your hands? You can use your outfits to highlight subtle or small aspects of your physical form. Adah says, "I like to try and accentuate how blonde I am in black and blues."

Once you've figured out what you want to highlight, you can spend some time identifying aspects you want to downplay. But be sure to ask yourself why you want to keep these particular traits out of sight. Is it because of something you've read, seen, or heard about how women's bodies should look? Or is it something you feel distracts from the parts of your body that you love and that steal the spotlight? Just because the media insists that big upper arms are "bad" doesn't mean you have to hide yours. These figure-flattery priorities are yours alone.

HIGHLIGHTING AND DOWNPLAYING

You get to decide if you want to make your bust look bigger or smaller, but you may need to know how to do one or both of those things. So here's your menu of figure-flattery basics:

How to Highlight Your Shoulders

- Cap sleeves end near shoulder level and will draw attention upward.
- Racerback tops might not work at school, but they show off more shoulder than most sleeveless styles.
- A boatneck or slash neck top will make your shoulders look broader.

How to Downplay Your Shoulders

- A deep V-neck will draw the eye away from broad or narrow shoulders.
- If you want to balance broad shoulders, a full skirt will do so by adding volume to the lower half of your body.
- Patterned pants or skirts will focus attention away from your upper body.

How to Highlight Your Bust

- Pendant necklaces naturally point toward and draw attention to the bust.
- Detailed necklines—interesting shapes or styles with embellishment—keep the focus up top.
- If you'd like to add volume to your bust, try a cowl neckline.

How to Downplay Your Bust

- Medium and large prints can distract from bust proportions. Small ones may do the opposite!
- Scoop necklines that fall above the cleavage line help balance a bust. High necklines and turtlenecks can make your bust look bigger or out of proportion.
- Sleeveless tops with a scoop neck or V-neck expose skin elsewhere on your top half and draw attention away from your bust.

Blending style tricks can draw the viewer's eye where you want it to be. For example, in this boho outfit, the deep V-neck draws the eyes away from the shoulders while the necklaces keep the focus on the top part of the dress.

FIGURING OUT YOUR FIGURE

How to Highlight Your Arms

- Sleeveless tops and dresses are the easiest way to show off arms.
- A pile of bracelets or one big bangle will attract attention to arms.
- A vest or other sleeveless garment worn over a long-sleeved top will draw the eye toward your arms.

How to Downplay Your Arms

- Three-quarter sleeves work beautifully. If you're worried about large arms, the three-quarter sleeve ends at a spot that's typically slimmer than the upper arm. If you're worried about slender arms, the three-quarter sleeve covers the arm nearly to the wrist, creating a modest look.
- Batwing, drapey, or kimono-style sleeves will mask arm size and shape entirely.
- Wearing bright shoes or patterned pants will train the focus downward and away from your arms.

This top, with a V-neck and shoulder straps, draws attention upward to the shoulders and collarbone and away from the bust. It's also a great choice for highlighting the arms.

How to Highlight Your Midsection

- Colorful, detailed, or patterned belts are ideal for attracting attention toward your waist.

- Fit-and-flare dresses nip in at the waist, showing it off.
- If you cuff your sleeves so that they hit at your waist when your arms are at your sides, you'll focus attention there.

How to Downplay Your Midsection

- A large necklace will draw the eye toward your face and away from your midsection.
- A tunic or top that hits mid-thigh worn with skinny pants or leggings puts the focus on your legs.
- A structured jacket or blazer will cover your waist without adding bulk to your silhouette.

How to Highlight Your Hips

- Skinny jeans and pants show off your lower half.
- Choose a top that ends right at your hips, and wear it with a contrasting bottom.
- A hip-slung belt worn over jeans or a dress puts the focus on your hips.

How to Downplay Your Hips

- Flared skirts and dresses—including fit-and-flare, A-line, and Empire-waist styles—will skim your hips without clinging.

A wide belt is a great choice for long-waisted figures.

FIGURING OUT YOUR FIGURE

- Boatnecks balance broad hips by adding visual volume to the shoulders.
- Bootleg or flared jeans also create balance by adding volume toward your feet.

How to Highlight Your Butt

- Cropped cardigans and jackets hit high on the body, allowing the butt to take center stage.
- Detailed back pockets on jeans or pants will draw attention.
- Skinny jeans and pants will show off both hips and butt.

How to Downplay Your Butt

- Dark-colored bottoms make your lower half less noticeable.
- A-line skirts and dresses will skim your butt. (Pencil skirts will cling, and full skirts may add volume.)
- Detailed necklines and eye-catching necklaces will keep attention toward your face.

How to Highlight Your Legs

- Any skirt or dress that's shorter than a maxi will show off your legs.
- Bright or patterned tights are a fun way to draw attention.

Choosing pants with a flared or bootleg cut is a simple trick for adding volume at the bottom of your outfit to balance or downplay shapely hips.

- A dark-colored top worn with a light-colored bottom will direct focus to your legs. (A light-colored top worn with a dark-colored bottom will direct focus upward.)

How to Downplay Your Legs

- Maxi skirts cover legs entirely and can downplay big or small legs.
- Pants with straight or wide-leg shapes make it harder to discern your leg shape.
- A light-colored top, scarf, or necklace that draws attention toward your face will keep the focus away from your lower half.

Several style features in this fun dress draw the eye downward and achieve additional goals. The dark bodice above the lighter, patterned skirt draws the focus away from the top and to the legs. So does the length of the skirt. And the Empire waist, ending just under the bust, is a way to minimize the hips.

UNDERNEATH IT ALL

Let's talk about bras and panties. Because even though very few people get to see your underwear, it has a huge impact on your figure and outfits.

Think about it. If you're wearing a slim-fitting dress with panties that cut into your waist or upper thighs, they will interrupt the curves of your figure. If your bra doesn't give your breasts enough support, it will change how your tops and dresses look and fit and how you can move when you are exercising. Underwear needs to be comfortable, but it also has a job to do. It needs to help your body look and feel its best underneath your clothes.

FIGURING OUT YOUR FIGURE

FIGURE-FLATTERY CHEAT SHEET

Here are a few other considerations to help with figure flattery:

The rule of thirds. If you wear jeans with a long top that covers your whole butt and visually cuts your body in half, you'll create proportions that make your legs seem short and your torso seem long. You'll also look a little more symmetrical than most female bodies do in nature. Ideally, you want your clothes and accessories to divide your body into thirds. That can mean a top (⅓), a skirt (⅓), and your exposed legs (⅓) or a top that hits mid-hip (⅓) and pants (⅔) or a dress (⅔) and your exposed legs (⅓) or a head scarf (⅓), a long dress (⅓) and a sweater (⅓).

Hems and breaks. The eye is drawn to the places where clothing stops—the end of your sleeve, the hem of your skirt, or the place where your boot hits your ankle or calf. If you want attention focused on a specific part of your body, place a visual break there. For instance, if you wear a white top and a black skirt, they'll make a high-contrast break at your waist and draw attention there.

Understanding color. Entire books have been written about figuring out which colors work with your skin tone, but here's the sound bite: If a color makes you look sick and pale or dulls your eye or hair color, consider wearing it away from your face. Colors that look great on you will make your face look healthy and your hair and eyes look bright. Of course, you can wear any color you like anywhere within your outfit! But if you've noticed that certain colors make you look unhealthy *and* it bothers you, wear those colors in shoes, bags, or pants instead of shirts and dresses.

Figure-flattery tips can be easy to put into action if you know how. These two women use color, balance, and the rule of thirds in different yet equally flattering ways. The woman on the right, for example, balances colors with a cropped sweater, skinny jeans, and open-toed wedge sandals. The woman on the left uses black-and-white contrast for a balanced look.

FIGURING OUT YOUR FIGURE

When it comes to panties, the pretty ones might not be the best ones. Lacy, sexy, sheer bottoms are lovely to look at, but if they pinch or subdivide your lower half they don't fit you properly. In fact, any underwear you buy and wear should sit flat and quiet against your body without pinching or digging. This means you may need to size up from what the packaging says. Your pants size and your underwear size aren't always the same. For instance, I wear a size 10 or 12 in pants and typically buy size XXL panties.

Explore various styles of panties too. You may need a shape that hits higher or lower on your torso to look and feel right. Explore bikinis, high-cuts, hipsters, boy shorts, and any other style you can find. Try them on (over your current underwear for sanitary reasons), and see how they interact with your body.

And bras? Oh, bras are so very tricky. It doesn't matter if your breasts are small or large, if you've had any kind of breast surgery or illness that affects their size and shape, or if you're struggling with how to highlight or downplay your breasts as part of your transition. We all struggle to understand these confounding bits of lingerie. So if possible, try to get professionally fitted for a bra. Measuring yourself can backfire, and working with a lingerie expert will help you figure out what size you wear and what style will work best for your frame and breast shape. Most major department stores will give you a free fitting. Just head to the lingerie department, and ask anyone who works there if you

A professional bra fitting can make all the difference between looking great in your clothes and feeling awkward or downright uncomfortable. Ask for a professional fitter at your favorite department store. Some lingerie shops have fitters on staff too. Or check online for how to measure yourself at home to make sure you purchase the best-fitting bra possible.

can be fitted for a bra. The salesperson will usually look at you in your bra and will want to see how the various bras she brings for you to try on are fitting you. If it helps, bring your mom or sister or best friend. And remember: This gal who is helping you find the right bra has seen more boobs than you could possibly imagine. She doesn't want to embarrass you, and she probably doesn't have any thoughts about your breasts other than, "Probably a 34C balconette for her."

A properly fitting bra will help your posture and support your breasts in a comfortable way. It will also positively impact how you look inside your clothes. Left to our own devices, most women pick the wrong bra size, so see if you can find a way to get fitted by a pro. And if you're someone who may not want to seek help in person at a major department store, lingerie online stores such as Bare Necessities and Figleaves have detailed measuring guides and a huge variety of cup and band sizes.

Finally, let's talk shapewear (a.k.a. Spanx). If you're going to a dance or a wedding and have a particular outfit that looks better when you pull on some shapewear, go for it. But studies have proven that wearing these undergarments all the time can negatively affect your internal organs and overall health. Because they're designed to be tight, they squeeze everything in your abdomen, from your stomach and intestines to your diaphragm and important nerves. While you're wearing it, shapewear can cause heartburn and belching. If you wear your Spanx all the time, you may end up with uncomfortable gas pains, heartburn, digestive issues, or numbness in your legs. Yikes! Shapewear is for special occasions. If you feel you need to wear it every single day to look your best, consider talking to someone about other ways to boost your body confidence. You can find many ways to look good and to feel confident without stressing your internal organs.

DRESS TO FEEL GOOD

Grace shared this story:

I remember this one time when I was in sixth grade I was at a store and I saw a tight, stretchy, fit-and-flare style dress that I had seen my friend wearing. I tried it on, and it looked AWFUL on me, because it made everything that's not completely flat on my upper body stand out while accentuating the fact that I had really small breasts. I remember being a little bit disappointed because my friend had looked so great in that dress, but the thing that we all have to come to accept is that there is clothing out there for everyone, and you have to find what makes you feel comfortable.

And she's right. Styles that look amazing on your friends might look odd on you. You do not have to wear what everyone else is wearing. You do not have to wear what's trendy. And most of all, you do not have to dress to make yourself look tall and thin and hourglass-like, no matter what the media may tell you.

You—and only you—pick your own dressing and figure-flattery priorities. Dress in clothes that make you feel good about yourself. Because those are the *only* clothes that deserve to adorn your unique and wonderful body.

CHAPTER 4
OUTFIT ASSEMBLY

Somewhere, someone must be working on an outfit creation app. With it you could upload photos of your clothes, tick a few boxes, and watch as an absolutely perfect group of items is assembled just for you and right before your eyes. I'd pay good money for it and use it daily.

Since outfit assembly is still a manual process, we might as well learn to be amazing at it.

PICK A STARTING POINT

You've got to start somewhere, and you are in charge of your outfit's starting point.

You can create an outfit from an emotional priority. For example, do you want to feel serene today? Powerful? Protected? Start with an item that aligns with your feelings and build from there. Colette in Iowa uses this technique. "I start with my confidence level that morning. If I'm feeling powerful and like a conqueress, I'll start with the center, typically my stomach. That always determines if I'll wear a dress or a miniskirt or a shirt. I don't know how, but I feel like building from the middle, then up and then down, works best for me."

You can create an outfit with a particular activity in mind. Do you need an outfit that will keep you dry on a long, rainy walk to soccer practice? Do you need to look a little fancier than usual for yearbook photos? Do you need to be all in black so you can go directly to theater crew after school? Start with an item that is essential to a particular activity, and build from there. Mollie often takes this route. "I start with a piece I know I need . . . it can be a shirt or something as small as a bracelet. Then I work from there."

You can also create an outfit by starting with a single item that you definitely want to wear on that particular day. This is how most outfits are born. A cozy sweater, a flowing maxi skirt, a colorful head scarf, or a killer pair of boots calls to you from the closet and becomes the jumping-off point for an entire outfit.

You can look to your mood to help you decide what to wear. For example, this young woman has chosen an edgy look, with a black top, leggings, and heavy boots. She signals her upbeat mood with a light blue knitted cap. It adds great visual pop too.

Jenna creates her outfits this way:

> I usually start with a top or a sweater that I want to wear, but I can change it up. Like today I found these jeans that are a really bright print so I was like, 'I wanna wear these and match them with this top.' I have to find a focus, what I want to be the 'bam!' of my outfit.

Once you've got a sense of your personal figure-flattery priorities and you know that dressing to feel great trumps all else, you can move on to the next steps of outfit creation.

DRESS FOR HAPPINESS

Have you ever noticed that when you wear bright colors in the dead of winter you get a ton of compliments? Or that a bad day can be made better by throwing on your favorite pair of shoes? What you wear can affect your mood, and you can choose to boost your happiness levels by selecting items that inspire joy.

Color is the big one and can instantly impact your state of mind. Which colors lift your spirits? Bold reds or cool blues? Do bright yellows or warm oranges energize you? Even if your favorites fail to flatter your coloring, wearing them in pants, shoes, or accessories can provide a mood boost.

Textures can inject happiness into your outfits too. Think about wearing cozy, soft cashmere or smooth, slippery silk. Imagine leaving the stiff denim jeans behind and slipping on a comfy pair of cotton leggings. Which textures make you feel alert and alive?

Whimsical, elegant, or quirky prints and patterns can help you feel more upbeat. Think of a shirt covered in tiny dogs wearing hats or a skirt with images of far-off constellations. Prints and patterns can cheer you up and spark your imagination. Sontra is a fan of florals. "I love colorful floral prints and when I wear them, they make me feel happy. It's fun to wear colorful clothing."

If you're hoping to dress for happiness, use color, texture, or print as your starting point and build your outfit from there.

DRESS FOR SELF-EXPRESSION

How you dress—your style, grooming, and overall appearance—are among the first things that everyone sees. Knowing that and working with it can give you a lot of power. You can choose which aspects of your personality, culture, gender identity, size, or other feature of who you are you want to express through your outfits, which trends to support, and which statement-making items to wear. You can show your love for your favorite sports team or band with a graphic tee, embrace your edgy side with combat boots or a leather jacket, or craft a neutral statement about gender through a marvelously androgynous look for yourself. You've got to get dressed every day anyway. Why not take the opportunity to show the world who you are through your personal style?

We can use clothes to make powerful statements about gender, whether we choose to announce the gender with which we identify, downplay it, opt for gender-neutral dressing, or mix and match feminized and masculinized elements.

OUTFIT ASSEMBLY

CREATING BALANCE IN YOUR OUTFITS

One of the most important elements of a stellar outfit is balance. The main types of balance are volume balance, color balance, and accessory balance.

Volume. This type of balance has to do with how much space a garment takes up on your body. An oversized sweatshirt is high volume, while skinny jeans are low volume. If you wear many high-volume items in the same outfit, you will look bigger than you actually are. Think of someone in a bulky, thigh-length sweater and wide-legged pants. All that volume will swallow up the wearer, hiding how she is really shaped. For a more balanced look, put volume in half of your outfit and slimness in another. For example, wear your oversized sweatshirt with your skinny jeans. Or put the volume on your bottom half by wearing a full, pleated skirt and pairing it with a fitted, shaped sweater on top.

Color. This type of balance within an outfit creates unity. Imagine someone wearing a bright red shirt, black pants, and black shoes. That is a two-chunk outfit, and the chunks have no visual relationship with each other. That same outfit with the addition of a black necklace? Much more balanced. Black now appears in both the top and bottom halves, which unifies the two main parts of the outfit.

You may have heard the phrase "pop of color," which means wearing a single item in a contrasting color somewhere within your outfit. This can be a fun technique to create off-kilter looks or to draw attention

This outfit works well because it balances volume (loose shirt on top, skinny jeans on the bottom) with color. The hijab and the jeans are both in the blue family, unifying the outfit. The peach-colored shirt adds a visual pop that pulls it all together.

to a specific part of your outfit and may be something you want to explore. But if you feel your outfit is disjointed somehow, see if balancing your color mix helps create more continuity.

Accessories. When you're adding accessories to an outfit, limit yourself to one big piece per area of the body. For instance, if you wear superlong earrings and a giant statement necklace, you've got two big, attention-grabbing accessories competing for attention near your face. It creates a confusing look. A long necklace that ends at your navel and a big wide belt will clack noisily against each other and fight for visual attention. A bright oversized scarf and a wide embellished headband create a hog pile of accessories.

If you want to go big, make sure your big piece stands alone. Do a statement necklace with stud earrings, a big wide belt with a shorter pendant necklace, or an oversized scarf with a headband-free hairdo. Balancing your accessories will help your outfits look sophisticated and complete.

Grace supports this philosophy, saying, "I think that fashion is a great way for people to express themselves and their personalities when people are dressing for themselves as opposed to dressing in order to satisfy others. I use clothing to express myself, and when other women use clothing to express themselves in a different way, it doesn't really bother me."

If you want to dress for self-expression, decide which parts of your inner life you want to share with the world, and build your outfit from there.

DRESS FOR COMFORT

I'll level with you. I don't think everyone should wear clothing with pajama-level comfort all the time. A little structure and formality to your outfits keeps you alert and focused. On the other hand, if you're wearing a jacket that pulls under the arms or a skirt that cuts into your midsection, you're not going to look or feel your best either.

Most of us have comfort priorities. You may not care as much about your waist, but you may absolutely require comfortable shoes for your fussy feet. Or maybe you're immune to itchy wool but cannot stand the feeling of tight pants. What are your personal comfort-related absolutes? Feet? Midsection? Texture? Which items in your closet accommodate these needs? Is there anywhere you could compromise so your outfit is comfy but not sloppy?

Mollie focuses on comfort. She says, "I like looking nice and feeling nice. But I put feeling nice before looking nice because it's what's more important. Comfort and self-expression are really intertwined to me."

If you want to dress for comfort, consider your top comfort priorities and build your outfit from there.

DRESS FOR POWER

Queens have crowns, superheroes have capes, and politicians have tailored suits. When people want to broadcast power, they tend to gravitate toward specific items of clothing and certain types of accessories. They skip sweatpants in favor of pencil skirts, swap cotton for leather, abandon blue for black, or swap pink for red. You too can create outfits that make you feel powerful. And there are different types of power to think about.

Power dressing usually relates to color, structure, and embellishment. Red and black are traditionally considered to be powerful colors, but any bold or bright color can convey power. You'll see politicians and other public figures choosing bright colors, often in fabrics without distracting patterns. Stiff fabrics such as wool and leather tend to appear more powerful than fluid fabrics such as silk or jersey. Businesswomen may choose to wear a silk blouse, for example, but they will usually pair it with a suit and jacket in a stiffer fabric. Metal embellishments such as spikes and studs exude toughness. They may not be appropriate in every situation, but in some cases, they can be just right. Kitana says, "My studded black boots make me feel powerful. I've had them since sophomore year and I'm never gonna get rid of them. They're my babies."

59

Somber colors such as black and gray send a message of power and authority, especially if they are coordinated in a suit ensemble.

Do you see a common thread here? Pastel colors, soft fabrics, and embroidery—all of which are usually associated with traditionally feminine forms of dressing—are not usually utilized in the United States to convey power. Bright colors, tough fabrics, and military patterns do send a message of power. In the world of dressing and fashion, feminine is traditionally viewed as weak while masculine is viewed as strong.

Yet many people choose to ignore or rebel against these conventions. If you enjoy dressing in masculine styles and want to take advantage of their power, do it. For decades women have worn clothing styles originally designed for men, and they have done so for many reasons: to rebel against social norms, to enjoy the comfort of menswear over the restrictions of women's wear, to express sexual preferences or gender identity, and to push against conventional ideas of what it means to be female. Men are increasingly embracing traditional women's fashions too. Fashion designers are offering skirts and dresses for men, and gender-neutral clothing is increasingly available at mall stores such as Zara and Selfridges. Young men are also experimenting with styling their long hair into buns.

You may feel perfectly comfortable with conventional norms of how to dress as a female and how to dress as a male. It's your call. But you can also choose to subvert the paradigm. You can choose to wear whatever makes you as an individual feel strong and mighty, and powerful and centered. Your power outfit might be a structured blazer, men's trousers, and a pair of oxford shoes; military fatigues with a pink tee; or a cardigan and a tulle skirt. Teen musician Jaden Smith wore a skirt to his prom in 2015. His date, actor Amandla Stenberg of *Hunger Games* fame, wore a traditional long evening gown. Jenna takes control of her image, saying:

What makes me feel powerful is if I wear what I like to wear.

CHAPTER 5

SHIFTING STYLE ON A BUDGET

If you've already got a wardrobe brimming with items that flatter your figure and express your personality, you are way ahead of the game. If you've got a wardrobe brimming with stuff you're not sure you want to wear anymore, don't panic. It is possible to shift your style and add new pieces to your closet without going on a mad mall spending

Thrift shopping is fun, and it can build your wardrobe without having to spend a lot of money.

spree. You can find ways to shop smart and affordably to fill out your wardrobe with figure-flattering clothes.

THE WONDERS OF SECONDHAND SHOPPING

Buying lots of inexpensive new clothes is fun at first. Mall and big-box stores have cute, trendy items at prices you can afford, and it can be hard to resist their lure. But you may have noticed that those five-dollar T-shirts and twelve-dollar jeans fall apart pretty quickly. And even worse, the manufacturers that make those clothes so cheaply do so by hiring women and children in poor nations and paying them far less than minimum wage. The laborers also often work long hours in unsafe conditions. And the factories use chemicals and fuels that harm the environment. That's all pretty depressing.

SHIFTING STYLE ON A BUDGET

Luckily, there's a fantastic alternative: thrift shopping. When you shop at secondhand stores, you are doing so many good things at once:

- You are practicing a form of recycling by reusing a garment that someone else has donated, and you are thereby extending the life of the clothing item.
- You are paying prices that are generally lower than in mall stores, so they are prices you can probably afford.
- You are supporting charities with your shopping dollars. Many thrift stores give a big percentage of their profits to organizations that help people in need. Many of these organizations provide job training to disabled or underprivileged people.
- You are shopping a mix of garments that often includes very high-quality clothes. When you find and buy these, you're taking home garments that will typically last longer than fast-fashion items bought brand new.
- You are accessing a varied pool of items that will help you look unique and different from folks who shop exclusively at the mall. Thrift stores sell a wide range of styles, unlike mall stores, which tend to focus on of-the-moment looks.

Seventeen-year-old Rain in Pennsylvania is a thrift shopping fan. She says:

> I shop at thrift stores a lot. I love being able to get $700 worth of clothes for typically under $100. And it's stuff no one wears anymore [so it helps me stand out].

Colette agrees. "I don't think there is any reason to *not* shop at a thrift store. There are thousands of possibilities and no set style. And you can customize anything you want because the prices are so low."

If charity-run, donations-only thrift stores overwhelm you, there are lots of other ways to buy great clothes secondhand such as these:

Garage, yard, and stoop sales. Most of the items your neighbors want to sell will be things like furniture, garden tools, and old CDs. But you can find some amazing clothing and jewelry if you're willing to make the rounds on Saturday mornings or go to sales in other neighborhoods in your town.

Consignment shops. Depending on the neighborhood, items at this type of store are usually more expensive than what you'll see at thrift shops, and here's why. People bring in their stuff, buyers sort through it and pick out the most recently made and coolest pieces, and only those items are put on the racks. So the selection may be smaller and more expensive but usually better quality. Use timing to your advantage. Items that are in the store for longer than a few weeks are usually discounted significantly. And look for sales at consignment shops. Many have regular sales where everything in the store goes for 50 percent off.

eBay. This online auction site has everything from vintage leather jackets to last year's prom dresses to gorgeous hijabs to barely used jeans. Read entries carefully, since many items are not returnable, but keep eBay in mind as a great secondhand shopping resource.

Online consignment outlets. If you do a quick search for "online consignment," you'll find at least a dozen great sites to explore. Many of them focus on designer goods only, but quite a few will offer you gently worn clothes, shoes, and accessories from your favorite mall stores. Many will include clothes that offer more coverage like maxi skirts and long-sleeved blouses. Check the rules for who can buy and sell on these sites. If you are younger than eighteen, you may need an adult to help you make purchases.

LEARNING TO LOVE HAND-ME-DOWNS

Being forced to wear your big sister's castoffs or the pants your cousin has outgrown can be kind of depressing. You want to create your own style, not dress in clothes that someone else picked out for herself and handed off to you when she was bored or they didn't fit.

The key to loving hand-me-downs is to focus on how you style them. Say you inherit a striped sweater from your sister. She wore it with skinny jeans and ballet flats. If you wear it with boyfriend jeans and sneakers or with cargo pants and a jean jacket or with a skirt and ankle boots, it will look completely different. Clothes are flat and lifeless on their own. They need your vision and creativity to make them sparkle and sing. Look at hand-me-downs and think, "How can I make these work for me?"

If you don't have an older sister or nearby cousins, think about the other women or maybe even the men in your family and life. Are you the same size as your mom or grandma? Does your brother have a shirt you really love? You might be able to inherit some fabulous pieces. Adah says, "My mom's youngest sister is two years older than me and I love her hand-me-downs. I don't like paying lots of money for clothes."

ACTIVITY: ONE SWEATER = THREE ACCESSORIES

Here's a super-easy way to make three accessories out of one old sweater:

WHAT YOU'LL NEED
- a pullover sweater with a pattern or a color you like, with some elasticity in it for making slightly stretchy accessories
- scissors
- a needle and thread
- decorations such as beads, fabric flowers, and colored thread

WHAT YOU'LL DO
1. On a work surface, lay your sweater out flat and cut the sleeve from the bodice, making sure your cut is parallel with the line formed by the bottom of the cuff. Hem the seam where you cut, and you have leg warmers. Keep the smaller end, which was once near the wrist, at your ankles and pull up from there.

2. With your sweater still lying flat, cut a 2- to 4-inch (5- to 10-centimeter) band from around the neckline. Hem on all sides, stitch the ends together, and you've just made a headband. Sew on beads or other small baubles to decorate.

3. Cut off the bottom half of the sweater, starting just below the armholes. Hem the seam you've just cut and you've got a circle scarf!

SHIFTING STYLE ON A BUDGET

THRIFT SHOPPING TIPS

If you're new to thrift shopping, vintage, consignment, and thrift shops can seem overwhelming. Some are organized by color, others by size, and a few appear to have no organization whatsoever. Here are some practices that will keep you focused and make your thrifting trips more fruitful. But remember: If you don't find what you want or like on one shopping trip, you don't have to buy anything. Ask the salesperson when a new shipment of items is due, and come back another day. The selection may include something you really love!

Bring a list. If you have a few items in mind, you can concentrate on tracking them down and skip over a few racks and departments. Try to keep your list pretty general. You'll have better luck finding "black sweaters" than you will finding "black cashmere V-necks with ribbed edging." Think categories more than items.

Tackle one department or section of a store at a time. Start with tops. Once you've got an armload, head to the fitting rooms and pick your favorites. Next, tackle the jackets. Hit the fitting rooms again. If you attempt to look through all the racks in all the departments before you try anything on, you'll exhaust yourself. Shop department by department instead.

A smart way to shop any thrift store is to break it up into manageable sections. Start on the first floor with whatever item you're looking for. Then move on to other sections, or other floors, one step at a time. You'll shop more efficiently this way.

If you're shopping for complete outfits, you can try for two departments in one round—blouses and skirts or sweaters and pants—before heading to the fitting rooms. Be flexible. You may not find coordinating pieces for an outfit in the same shopping trip. But if you totally love one of the items and the price is right, buy it and come back later—or shop elsewhere—to find just the right piece to go with it.

Examine every item carefully. Depending on the store, most donated or consigned items are in amazing shape. But some stores sell items that are stained or torn or missing buttons or zippers or full of moth holes. Before you plunk down your cash, take a long, hard look at every inch of your potential purchases. Think about what you could easily fix and what you can't. A button missing? Buttons are easy to find and if you or a friend has basic sewing skills, buttons are easy to sew onto a garment. A seam missing a few stitches? That's easy to fix too. But if there's a giant rip or tear in the back of a dress, that's probably not something you or anybody else can fix. The same is true for stains and odors. They can be almost impossible to get rid of.

Buy for fit and function. What this really means is DON'T buy something because it's a covetable brand name. DON'T buy something because it's cool and cheap if it doesn't fit well or you have nowhere to wear it. It will end up in the back of your closet, and you will have wasted money on something you never wear.

Don't let the size tag turn you off. Thrifting will teach you that size tags are meaningless. If something looks like it might fit, try it on, regardless of the marked size. If an item has European sizing (in the 30s or 40s), judge by whether the piece looks as if it might fit or ask the salesperson to help you understand what the equivalent US size is. Different manufacturers use different sizing systems, so don't let the numbers dictate whether an item will fit or not. Trust your own judgment.

Keep an open mind. Even if you thrift with a list of things to look for, be open to hidden gems. If that suede jacket is calling your name, see if it fits. If the shoulder bag in the corner isn't on your list, but it's the style or the brand you've been looking for since last year, grab it. Being a focused thrift shopper is important, but so is going with the flow.

SHIFTING STYLE ON A BUDGET

What about your friends? Invite them over on a weekend afternoon and tell everyone to bring a bag of cast-off clothes. Lay everything out on a big table and start swapping. Your bestie might be sick to death of that skirt, but it could be totally perfect for you.

SEW, REPURPOSE, AND TAILOR

To revise your look, you don't always need to bring new items into your closet. If you're at all crafty, consider a few simple sewing projects. Circle skirts and short-sleeved tops are relatively easy to whip up using easy patterns. Once you know your measurements and feel confident at the sewing machine, you can start tackling dresses, pants, jackets, and other items that can be made from a pattern. Patterns are easy and inexpensive to find online or at your favorite fabric store. And sewing your own clothes has many advantages. If you have trouble finding clothes that fit, for example, creating them yourself means they'll be customized to your exact measurements. You get to choose the type of cloth, color, and print you want. And you'll be creating garments that no one else in the world has.

If sewing from scratch doesn't appeal to you, you can choose from several fun and easy ways to repurpose some of the clothes you have. Old jeans can become cutoff shorts with a few scissor snips. You can embellish plain tees, dresses, skirts, pants, and jackets with sequins, embroidery, rhinestones, or fabric paint. Create your own slogan shirts with iron-on letters. Make leg warmers from sweater sleeves, or put together infinity scarves from the hems of old dresses. There are more repurposing projects than you could imagine. Ask your friends for ideas, or do some quick searches on Google or Pinterest to drum up more ideas and to find tutorials.

TAILORING TIPS

Tailors can fix many clothing issues, but not all of them. Keep these things in mind before taking your items to the tailor's shop.

TAILORS/ALTERATION SHOPS CAN DO THIS

- Shorten just about anything. Pants, skirts, and dresses can be shortened at the hem. Dresses and jackets can be shortened at the sleeves. Jackets can sometimes be shortened, but this alteration is generally expensive because it usually involves taking the entire garment apart, adjusting it, and putting it back together again.

- Make most garments smaller. Tops, dresses, pants, skirts, and just about every other garment can be taken in. You can also have garments reshaped. Boxy tops can be altered to nip at the waist, and straight-leg jeans can be made into skinnies. That said, taking a size 14 dress to a tailor and requesting it be taken in to fit your size 6 frame will generally backfire. And even if it works, it'll be expensive.

TAILORS/ALTERATION SHOPS CANNOT DO THIS

- Make something significantly longer. If a skirt, dress, or pair of pants has an allowance (extra fabric at the hemline), the tailor might be able to squeeze an extra half inch (1.3 cm) out of it. The sleeves of tops and jackets can sometimes be slightly lengthened, but the bodies of these garments are unlikely to yield any extra length.

- Do much with sweaters. Unless you're dealing with boiled wool or some other very stiff, fabric-like knit, sweaters can't be changed. So buy carefully!

- Make something bigger. There usually isn't enough allowance in the hems to make something more than an inch (2.5 cm) bigger. The rule of thumb is that it's much easier to make big smaller than to make small bigger.

Some tailors focus their businesses on specialties such as suiting, and others prefer complex jobs for which they can charge higher fees. So certain shops may be unwilling to shorten all of your beloved graphic tees. Ask family and friends for recommendations, or call ahead and ask if a certain tailor will take on your alterations. Most will be happy to help, but it's better to be sure ahead of time!

SHIFTING STYLE ON A BUDGET

If you have a few items that are just shy of perfect, consider taking them to a professional tailor or an alteration shop. If your favorite jeans gap at the waist, they can be taken in. If your best sweatshirt's sleeves are too long, they can be shortened. If you have a dress that's a size or two too big, a skilled seamstress can reshape it for you. (Tailoring and sewing are different skill sets. Creating a garment from scratch is often easier than figuring out why it doesn't fit correctly in one spot, then taking it apart, tweaking it, and putting it back together again. Many people who sew take their clothes to tailors and alteration shops for complex alterations.)

Tailoring and alterations aren't necessarily inexpensive, but they are often cheaper than buying an entirely new garment. Simple alterations such as hemming generally cost between ten and twenty dollars. More complicated projects such as shortening the sleeves on a lined jacket can get into the fifty- to sixty-dollar range. Tailoring isn't the perfect solution to every clothing issue, but it can sometimes raise a garment from good to perfect. Look online to see if there's an alteration shop in your neighborhood. Or maybe a friend or relative has sewing skills and can help you with the item you want to adjust.

THE POWER OF REMIXING

In the world of fashion, *remixing* is a term that's used loosely. To some, it means using the same pieces in a variety of outfits.

To others, it means using certain pieces in unusual and creative ways. Either way, you can find ways to concoct unusual outfits using items you already own without ever picking up a needle and thread.

Got an A-line or full-skirted dress that's too short? Try layering a slightly longer, lightweight skirt under it like a slip. Allow the hemline of the lightweight skirt to peek out and add length. Wish you had more skirts? Layer a sweater over one of your dresses to make it look like a skirt. Wear a tank top instead of a sweater vest over a button-front shirt or blouse. Use a thin scarf as a belt. Fold over the waistband of an elastic-waist skirt to shorten it. Scoot an oversized button-front shirt downward so the collar sits at the small of your back, tie the arms around your waist, and wear it as a skirt. And think about wearing your favorite red top with a black skirt one day and with gray trousers the next. You can play with accessories to further bolster the remixing of the same top from one day to the next. Use your imagination! Dream up new and different ways to wear the clothes that hang in your closet right now. You might find out that you don't need to buy a single new thing to create the wardrobe of your dreams.

SOURCE NOTES

10 Olivia, e-mail correspondence with author, November 1, 2014.

12 "5 of Our Favorite Things Zooey Deschanel (Glamour's February Cover Star!) Shared with Us," *Glamour*, January 2, 2013, http://www.glamour.com/story/5-of -our-favorite-things-zooey.

12 Jenna, interview with author, October 14, 2014.

13 "Kelly Clarkson on Weight Criticism: 'We Are Who We Are, Whatever Size,'" *People*, April 3, 2015, http://stylenews.people.com/style/2015/04/03/kelly-clarkson -talks-about-her-weight-on-ellen/.

15 Grace, e-mail correspondence with author, October 20, 2014.

15 Cameron Russell, "Looks Aren't Everything. Believe Me, I'm a Model," *TED*, October 2012, http://www.ted.com/talks/cameron_russell_looks_aren_t_ everything_believe_me_i_m_a_model?language=en.

16 Sontra, e-mail correspondence with author, October 31, 2014.

18–19 Alisha, e-mail correspondence with author, April 15, 2015.

23 Wrenna, e-mail correspondence with author, November 29, 2014.

26–27 Kitana, interview with author, October 14, 2014.

30 Adah, interview with author, October 25, 2014.

32 Alisha, e-mail correspondence with author, April 15, 2015.

32 Mollie, e-mail correspondence with author, October 26, 2014.

33 Olivia, e-mail.

35 Adah, interview.

39 Alisha, e-mail.

40 Adah, interview.

50 Grace, e-mail.

53 Colette, e-mail correspondence with author, December 8, 2014.

53 Mollie, e-mail.

54 Jenna, interview.

55 Sontra, e-mail.

58 Grace, e-mail.

58 Mollie, e-mail.

59 Kitana, interview.

Haute Hijab

http://www.hautehijab.com

This site began as a personal style blog for Melanie Elturk and has evolved into an online shop, community, and resource for Muslim women.

Inside Out Style

http://www.insideoutstyleblog.com/

This blog is written by an internationally certified image consultant with a wealth of knowledge about proportion, color, and outfit assembly.

Manufactured 1987

http://manufactured1987.com/

On this tumblr, disabled model and blogger Jillian Mercado posts behind-the-scenes shots from her campaigns and shares her thoughts on the fashion industry.

Mode-sty

http://www.mode-sty.com/

Mainly a shopping site aimed at women who need stylish clothes that offer more coverage, Mode-sty also has a blog that highlights high-fashion and celebrity styles and looks.

My Therapist Told Me to Write a Fashion Blog

http://mytherapisttoldmetowriteafashionblog.com/

Orthodox Jewish blogger and fashion writer Malky Weichbrod writes about and showcases style and beauty inspiration on this image-heavy tumblr.

P.S.—I Made This . . .

http://psimadethis.com/

Tutorials abound on this crafty, do-it-yourself blog, and the majority of them focus on fashion. Learn to make accessories from scratch, repurpose old clothes, and improve on wardrobe favorites.

Rookie

http://www.rookiemag.com/

Rookie is an online publication for teenage girls featuring writing, photography, illustrations, and videos from staff and readers. The site features monthly issues, each revolving around a theme, and offers content for girls of all sizes, ethnicities, genders, and faiths.

Thrift Shopper

http://www.thethriftshopper.com

Do you know where thrift shops are in your hometown? This national directory lets you search by zip code for secondhand shops in your area.

You Look Fab

http://youlookfab.com/

Click on the "Advice" tab of this blog to peek into the archive of posts covering figure-flattery basics. The author is a stylist with more than twenty years of experience.

Beauty Redefined

http://www.beautyredefined.net/

Run by identical twin sisters with PhDs in the study of media and body image, this site aims to help readers recognize harmful media messages, redefine ideas around beauty, and resist the notion that there is only one right way to be beautiful.

Budget Babe

http://www.thebudgetbabe.com

If you prefer to shop new, this popular blog focuses on the best picks from affordable stores such as Forever 21, Kohl's, Target, and T.J. Maxx. You'll also learn how to re-create celebrity outfits on a budget.

Curvy Fashionista

http://thecurvyfashionista.com/

This blog has multiple contributors writing about style and shopping for plus-sized girls, including many women of color and a petite-plus woman. The *Curvy Fashionista* is often the first website to break stories about new and exciting plus-size lines and designer collaborations.

dapperQ

http://www.dapperq.com

This website offers resources, articles, and industry coverage for anyone who gravitates toward traditionally male fashion. *dapperQ* includes great articles for queer and transgender individuals looking for shopping and styling advice.

Eff Your Beauty Standards

http://www.instagram.com/effyourbeautystandards/

Started by plus-size model Tess Holliday, this account is populated by women (and some men and gender-fluid individuals) who push back against the idea that there's only one way to be beautiful.

Geena Davis Institute on Gender in Media

http://seejane.org

Founded by Academy-Award-winning actor Geena Davis, the institute focuses on educating and inspiring content creators to focus on gender equality and to reduce stereotyping in media aimed at young people. The site is a great resource for informative articles, videos, and events about race, gender, stereotyping, and other issues that impact media portrayal of males and females.

Genderfork

http://genderfork.com

Although not specifically focused on style, *Genderfork* is an incredibly supportive community for the expression of identities across the gender spectrum. This site is a haven for anyone struggling with gender identity.

Gurl

http://www.gurl.com

This website provides a community in which teen girls can read about and discuss style, body image, sexuality, beauty, mental health, and more.

FURTHER INFORMATION

Books

Brashich, Audrey D. *All Made Up: A Girl's Guide to Seeing through Celebrity Hype and Celebrating Real Beauty*. New York: Walker, 2006. The author of this book is a former model and longtime media-awareness advocate. She passionately explores and explains how pop culture impacts self-esteem.

London, Stacy. *The Truth about Style*. New York: Penguin Books, 2013. In this book, the former cohost of TV's *What Not to Wear* opens up about her own body image and style journey. She also helps nine women understand their figures and learn to dress them well. Visual examples help reinforce figure-flattery concepts.

Molinary, Rosie. *Beautiful You: A Daily Guide to Radical Self-Acceptance*. Berkeley, CA: Seal, 2010. This book offers one focused task each day for an entire year, all designed to improve body image and build confidence.

Shoket, Ann, *Seventeen Ultimate Guide to Style: How to Find Your Perfect Look*. Philadelphia: Running Press, 2011. Much of the advice in this book focuses on creating outfits that make you look tall and thin. But it also includes great input from magazine editors, teen girls, and celebrity stylists for a well-rounded view of style. It will help readers explore classic, edgy, girly, glam, sporty, artsy, and boho styles and learn how to craft outfits for each.

Style Secrets series. Minneapolis: Lerner Publications, 2016. This four-book series for middle-grade readers offers creative, practical, do-it-yourself ways for tweens and teens to look their best, stay healthy, and flaunt their personal style. Each book contains numerous DIY activities, along with tips for taking good care of your body and your style supplies. Examples and beyond-the-basics information encourage readers to put their own spin on each book's style tricks.

What's Your Style? series. Minneapolis: Lerner Publications, 2014. Find out all about five hot fashion styles—from hipster to boho chic—in this fun series that profiles celebs who cultivate each look and who explain how tween and teen readers can make the look their own.

Websites

About-Face
http://www.about-face.org
This website focuses on giving girls and women the tools they need to understand and resist destructive media messages.

Already Pretty
http://www.alreadypretty.com
This blog focuses on the intersection of style and body image, responds to reader requests, shares shopping resources, and explains figure-flattery concepts.

61   Jenna, interview.

64   Rain, e-mail correspondence with author, November 2, 2014.

65   Colette, e-mail.

66   Adah, interview.

77   "Gabi Fresh Opens Up on Her Identity as a Plus-Size Woman," *Huffington Post*, last modified January 19, 2013, http://www.huffingtonpost.com/2013/01/17/gabi -freshidentity-plus-size-woman-_n_2499240.html.

SELECTED BIBLIOGRAPHY

Gruys, Kjerstin. *Mirror, Mirror off the Wall: How I Learned to Love My Body by Not Looking at It for a Year*. New York: Avery, 2013.

Kilbourne, Jean. *Can't Buy My Love: How Advertising Changes the Way We Think and Feel*. New York: Simon & Schuster, 2000.

Woodall, Trinny, and Susannah Constantine. *What You Wear Can Change Your Life*. New York: Riverhead Books, 2005.

INDEX

ABOUT THE AUTHOR

Sally McGraw is a Minneapolis-based freelance writer, editor, and blogger. She holds a creative writing degree from Binghamton University and spent ten years working in the book and magazine publishing industry before striking out on her own in 2011. In addition to writing her popular style and body image blog, *Already Pretty* (alreadypretty.com), she has published a style guide titled *Already Pretty: Learning to Love Your Body by Learning to Dress It Well*.

McGraw spent nearly a decade working as a personal stylist, currently writes a monthly style column for the *Minneapolis Star Tribune*, and contributes body image articles to the *Huffington Post*. She helps other writers find their voices through her freelance ghostwriting and editorial work. In her free time, she cochairs the board of an emerging women's leadership fellowship, scours eBay for secondhand fashion finds, and attempts to entertain her two kooky cats.